THE STORY OF THE FIRST WORLD WAR
OF THE

WORLD WAR

An Allied tank lumbers
through the battlefield of
Cambrai, France, in 1917.

The view from the front line, painted by
artist CRW Nevinson, shows common sights
from the Western Front: the barbed wire
used to snare attacking soldiers, artillery
shells exploding, and the poppies that would
become a poignant symbol of the War.

THE STORY OF THE FIRST WORLD WAR

Paul Dowswell

Designed by Tom Lalonde & Samantha Barrett

Illustrated by Ian McNee

Edited by Jane Chisholm   Managing designer: Stephen Moncrieff

Consultant: Simon Robbins, Historian, Imperial War Museums

Contents

1917: Cracks & catastrophes

1918: Collapse

1919: The flawed peace

An Allied soldier runs for cover during the Battle of Passchendaele, 1917. On either side of him are the shattered remains of a horse-drawn carriage caught by shellfire.

A Sopwith Camel fighter plane comes to a fatal end somewhere behind the Allied lines. This highly effective aircraft was used by British, French and US forces, but was notoriously difficult to fly, especially when taking off and landing.

The Great War

In August 1914, a global conflict broke out that was to last four and a quarter years, ending in November 1918. As it progressed, people spoke of it as the 'war to end all wars' or 'The Great War'. Although most of the fighting took place in Europe, it touched every corner of the world – from the South Atlantic in the West, to the ports of China in the East.

As many as 65 million men fought in the War, and 21 million people died, including 13 million civilians. Across Europe, almost every village and town has a memorial to their dead. Similar memorials can be found in Canada, Australia, New Zealand, India and the USA.

A map of the War

The First World War was fought between two great power blocs.
On one side were 'the Allies': Britain, France and Russia, joined
later by Italy and the USA; on the other, 'the Central Powers':
Germany, Austria-Hungary, Bulgaria and the Ottoman empire.
The battlefields ranged across the world, but the heaviest
fighting took place on either side of the German border, known
as the Eastern and Western fronts. But, as stalemate set in there,
the focus shifted to the Mediterranean, as well as European
colonial territories in the Middle East, Africa and Asia.

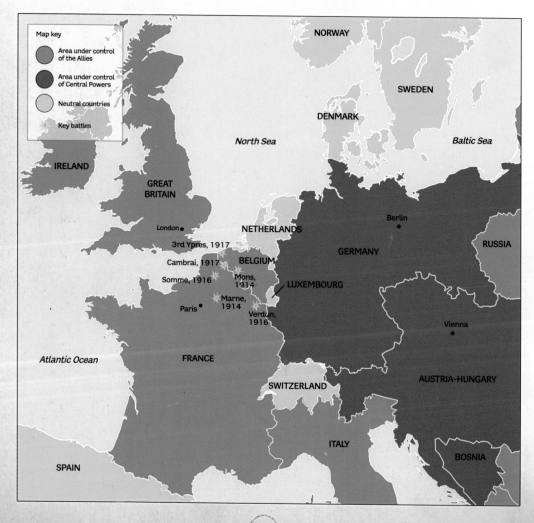

Map key
- Area under control of the Allies
- Area under control of Central Powers
- Neutral countries
- Key battles

NORWAY

SWEDEN

DENMARK

North Sea

Baltic Sea

IRELAND

GREAT BRITAIN

London

3rd Ypres, 1917

Cambrai, 1917

Somme, 1916

Paris

Berlin

NETHERLANDS

BELGIUM

Mons, 1914

LUXEMBOURG

Marne, 1914

Verdun, 1916

GERMANY

RUSSIA

Vienna

Atlantic Ocean

FRANCE

SWITZERLAND

AUSTRIA-HUNGARY

SPAIN

ITALY

BOSNIA

CANADA

UNITED STATES

Atlantic Ocean

RUSSIA

CHINA

INDIA

Pacific Ocean

Pacific Ocean

AUSTRALIA

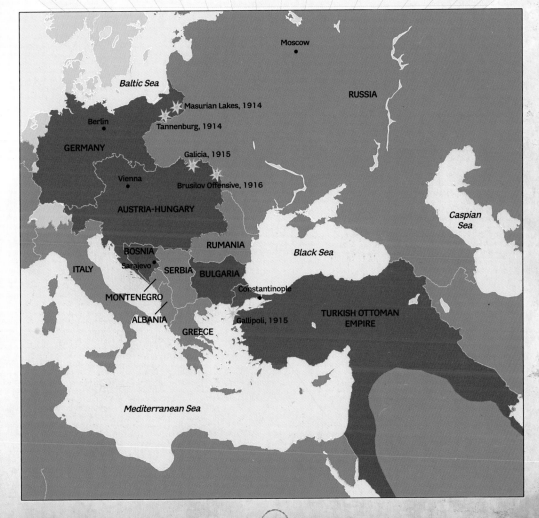

Moscow

Baltic Sea

RUSSIA

Masurian Lakes, 1914

Berlin

Tannenburg, 1914

GERMANY

Galicia, 1915

Vienna

Brusilov Offensive, 1916

AUSTRIA-HUNGARY

Caspian Sea

RUMANIA

Black Sea

BOSNIA

Sarajevo

ITALY

SERBIA

BULGARIA

MONTENEGRO

Constantinople

ALBANIA

TURKISH OTTOMAN EMPIRE

Gallipoli, 1915

GREECE

Mediterranean Sea

French cavalry watch a fighter plane fly by. The years before the First World War saw great advances in technology, not least in the killing power of weapons of war. Traditional fighting tactics were slow to adapt and the result was unprecedented slaughter.

Chapter 1

The build-up to war

The turn of the 20th century was a time of optimism and prosperity, of industrial and mechanical marvels – great factories, steamships and locomotives, and extraordinary new flying machines. Below the surface, however, there was seething political discontent: trade unions striking for better working conditions, women suffragettes demanding voting rights, terrorist assassinations and national rivalries. But the period may now be remembered more fondly, viewed across the abyss of 'the Great War' to come.

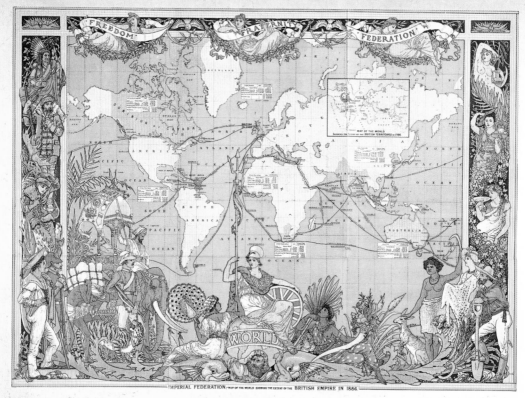

IMPERIAL FEDERATION—MAP OF THE WORLD SHOWING THE EXTENT OF THE BRITISH EMPIRE IN 1886.

The pink shaded areas on this Victorian world map show the extent of the British empire in 1866.

Fledgling superpower

In the decades following the American Civil War (1861-65), the USA grew wealthier and more powerful. The country was transformed by building a railroad network, and increases in agricultural and industrial production.

Industrialists such as John D. Rockefeller, Andrew Carnegie and J.P. Morgan made stupendous fortunes, and ten million immigrants, mostly from Europe, flocked to 'the land of opportunity'.

The Victorian world

At the beginning of the 20th century, Europe was the cultural and economic headquarters of the world. It had grown in prosperity in the second half of the 19th century, a period often described as the Victorian era, after the long-reigning monarch of the most powerful country of the day: Queen Victoria.

Industry and empire

Europe owed its prosperity to two key factors: industry and colonies. It was first to make use of steam power and to mass produce goods in factories. The USA and Japan were quick to follow. British textiles and other goods were sold all over the world, and Germany became a major exporter of chemicals – dyes and medicines.

Empire building

In the 19th century there had been a rush by European countries to seize uncolonized lands, particularly in Africa and Asia. By the time the First World War broke out in 1914, there were only two independent nations left in Africa: Ethiopia and Liberia.

These new colonies provided workers for factories, raw materials to be made into goods, and markets for the finished products manufactured in factories of 'the mother country'.

This wealth built many of the fine buildings in Europe's capital cities that we still admire today. The grandeur of Pall Mall and South Kensington in London, the Unter den Linden in Berlin, the Paris Opera – are all products of this age of opulence.

Unter den Linden (meaning 'under the lime trees'), in the middle of Berlin, proclaimed Germany's new confidence and prosperity. This photograph was taken in 1900.

Victoria: Europe's grandmother

Many of the royal families of Europe were closely related. George V of Britain, Kaiser Wilhelm II of Germany, and Tsar Nicholas II of Russia were all cousins, sharing a grandmother in Queen Victoria.

George V

Kaiser Wilhelm II

Tsar Nicholas II

This close blood relationship made many people feel Europe was safe from a large-scale war.

Dreadnoughts

Dreadnoughts were bigger, faster and more powerful than any warship before them. They made use of new technology – steam turbines, to power their propellers, which made them fast enough to travel nearly 600 miles (over 900km) in a day. Dreadnoughts had 10 big guns, each of which could fire a 390kg (850 lbs) shell over 10km (6 miles).

By 1914, Britain had 30 dreadnoughts, and the Germans had built 20. This rivalry was reaching breaking point.

Arms race

By the beginning of the 20th century, Europe's most powerful nations were split into two rival power blocs. Many royal families were closely related, and trade flourished across Europe, but there was still intense suspicion between the rival nations. People believed that if one side grew more powerful than the other, it would use that power to dominate Europe and war would become inevitable.

In 1910, a British writer, Norman Angell, published a book called *The Great Illusion*. In it he argued that war between European countries would never happen. Their economies were so closely linked, war would undermine the prosperity they all enjoyed. Angell thought the military might of opposing sides would make war so destructive it would be unthinkable. His book was hugely popular, but he was wrong about everything – apart from the catastrophic consequences of a war.

Wave power

Britain believed its prosperity and security rested on its Royal Navy. To maintain its position in the world, it was thought that its navy should be twice the size of any two rivals.

Germany, in turn, wanted more colonies, and Britain feared they might try to seize some of theirs. Both sides tried to outmatch the other by building warships to protect their overseas possessions, or help gain them further territories. Their biggest rivalry was in the race to build super battleships known as dreadnoughts.

We want eight!

Dreadnoughts were hugely expensive, even by today's standards, and the British government was forced to raise taxes to pay for them.

Despite this, many people were anxious for them to be built. Novels and articles predicting a German invasion were popular at the time. So when the government proposed to build only four new dreadnoughts, politicians were greeted by crowds of demonstrators chanting, "We want eight and we won't wait!"

When it was built in 1906, *HMS Dreadnought* was the fastest battleship in the world. It gave its name to a whole class of super battleships.

Shifting alliances

One major cause of the Great War was the system of alliances that had developed between the major European nations. Each one believed it was stronger and safer inside a partnership of allies. They hoped that the sheer size and strength of the two sides would prevent either one from attacking the other.

But this belief had a serious flaw. Some began to fear that if Germany became stronger it might tip this precarious balance of power. Then, when war came, opposing nations would be dragged into a conflict they had no interest in pursuing.

LE GRAND OGRE ALLEMAND.

A French cartoon of the 'giant German ogre', the German Chancellor Otto von Bismarck

A new nation

19th century Germany was made up of 39 small independent states. Prussia, the most powerful, persuaded the others to invade France in 1870, taking over Alsace and Lorraine, and to unite around Prussia to create a powerful new nation.

This painting shows Wilhelm I of Prussia being proclaimed *Kaiser* (meaning 'king') of the Germans, in the Hall of Mirrors, Versailles in 1871 – a key moment in the rise of German power.

Ententes and alliances

Fearing French retaliation after the Franco-Prussian War, the Germans made an alliance with Austria-Hungary, promising each other miltary aid if Russia or France attacked either of them. Italy joined in 1882, forming a triple alliance known as the Central Powers.

In the decades that followed, France, Russia and Britain also negotiated alliances amongst themselves, offering mutual aid if one or other was attacked. Finally, in 1907, all three came together in an agreement known as the *Triple Entente* (meaning 'agreement' or 'understanding').

Causes for war

One of the things that alarmed France, Britain and Russia most was the rise of German military officials to leading government positions. They were right to worry. War with France had united the new nation and won territory for it on France's eastern border. Now some members of the government began to push for further military adventures.

The Schlieffen Plan

Fearing a war on both the French and Russian fronts, Count Alfred von Schlieffen devised what he thought was a foolproof plan.

Believing the vast but sluggish Russian army would be slow to arrive at Germany's eastern border, he proposed to defeat France quickly by a surprise thrust through neutral Belgium. This would enable the German army to seize Paris, and defeat the French in six weeks.

Then the Germans could turn their full military strength on Russia. Schlieffen retired in 1905, but his plan gave German leaders false hope that they might win an easy victory. Without it, they might have been more cautious.

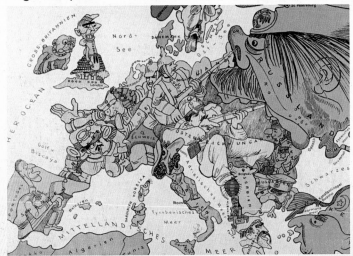

This German cartoon map of Europe, made in 1914, shows Germany (blue) and Austria-Hungary (yellow) as determined soldiers with weapons at the ready, surrounded by hostile powers.

Archduke Franz Ferdinand and his wife Sophie on June 28, the final day of their lives

Friendly foes

The First World War didn't seem inevitable at the time. Although rival nations nursed fears and resentments against each other, no one imagined how terrible the forthcoming conflict would be.

Even in 1913, the British and German monarchs attended military exercises dressed in each other's uniforms as a gesture of goodwill.

The fatal spark

The slide towards war began on June 28, 1914. The heir to the Austro-Hungarian throne, Archduke Franz Ferdinand, took his wife on a state visit to Sarajevo, the capital of Bosnia, a country recently annexed by the empire. But it was seen by many as a tactless gesture. Most Bosnians were loyal to their fellow Slav nation, Serbia, and many wanted Bosnia and Serbia to unite and break away from the Austro-Hungarian empire.

The Archduke and his wife were shot dead by 19 year-old Gavrilo Princip, a young student anarchist. The Austrians blamed the Serbs. Within a month, and with German backing, the Austrians had declared war on Serbia.

A chain reaction

But now the tangled web of great alliances exerted a fatal pull. Russia was an ally of Serbia's, and on July 31, the Russians began to mobilize their huge army to defend Serbia. They were preparing the army for war in case the Austro-Hungarians didn't back down. It wasn't a declaration of war in itself.

Germany feared the Russian army. It was slow and primitive, but vast and powerful too. German leaders spoke of their fear of 'the Russian steamroller'. They declared war on Russia, anxious to begin preparing for battle as soon as possible. In response, Russia's ally France began to prepare for war too. So Germany declared war on France, setting in motion the Schieffen Plan (see page 17).

A fatal miscalculation

On August 4, German troops invaded neutral Belgium, intending to conquer France quickly, and then turn their full might on Russia. They never expected the British to intervene. But the British feared that a German occupation of Belgian ports would threaten their control of the English Channel and their trade with Europe. So, citing an ancient treaty in which they promised to protect Belgium, the British declared war on Germany.

Many members of the British government didn't relish a war over what they referred to as 'a Balkan quarrel'. And the Germans, in turn, tried their best to reassure them that they had no hostile intentions. But, despite a series of frantic diplomatic meetings and telegrams, the entire continent was now at war.

War fever

News of war was greeted by delirious crowds in the capital cities of the major combatants. Each country was convinced the war would be over by Christmas.

The Kaiser went one better. His troops, he told them, would be home, "before the leaves left the trees." No one really knew what to expect. Apart from the brief Franco-Prussian War of 1870-71, the last major European war had happened 100 years before, with Napoleon. They were in for a terrible shock.

"No man in the prime of his life knew what war was like. All imagined that it would be an affair of great marches and great battles, quickly decided."

British historian AJP Taylor

Cheerful Parisians leave the French capital to join their army units in August 1914. Many of them will be killed in the first intense weeks of fighting.

Chapter 2

1914: Outbreak

The outbreak of war brought hundreds of thousands of patriotic young men flocking to army recruitment offices throughout Europe. But no one knew what awaited them. Each new recruit imagined he would be home within months, even weeks, perhaps with a glamorous minor injury to show for his gallant adventure.

Huge numbers of soldiers were killed in the opening weeks of the war. Within a month it was plain to see that the armies of Europe faced a new kind of warfare: one in which the defenders had an overwhelming advantage over the attackers. Ahead lay four years of slaughter on an industrial scale.

The Western Front

The War began as expected – with great marches and great ambitions. The French attacked their German border, hoping to reclaim territory in Alsace and Lorraine, that had been seized in 1871.

Their troops went into battle dressed traditionally and conspicuously in bright red and blue uniforms, with the cavalry in gleaming silver breastplates. Not surprisingly, they were cut down by German machine gunners. Casualties were horrific: by the end of the year 300,000 French soldiers had been killed and almost 700,000 injured. The bright uniform had to be changed to a duller blue.

Attack and counter-attack

General Helmuth von Moltke, the German commander, was determined to carry out Schlieffen's plan and attack France through Belgium. But there were problems from the start. The Belgians put up an unexpectedly strong resistance, and the Russians arrived faster than expected on Germany's eastern border.

Signal failure

In the West, the German High Command was plagued by communication problems. Their radio signals were jammed by electronic equipment installed at the top of the Eiffel Tower.

Worse, their signals were uncoded, so the French, who were listening, knew exactly where the next attack was coming from.

This massive swathe of soldiers advancing across open fields shows the German army in training just before the outbreak of war.

Days from Paris

By late August, the Germans were only days from Paris. A million Parisians fled, and the French government left for Bordeaux. Scenting victory, the German Chancellor composed a peace memorandum demanding vast amounts of money and territory from the French.

But at this crucial moment, a vigorous French counterattack on the Marne river hit exhausted German troops. By September 10, von Moltke abandoned his plan. He was reported to have told the Kaiser: "Your Majesty, we have lost the War."

Both sides hoped to outflank the other, but without success. By the end of the year, they faced each other along 765 km (475 miles) of fortified trenches – from the Channel to the Alps. The true nature of the War had revealed itself.

The 1st Battle of Ypres

The Battle of Ypres, fought in autumn rain and freezing mud at a small town near the Belgian coast, was a warning of things to come.

During October and November 1914, 50,000 German, and 25,000 Allied soldiers were killed. The British army lost many of its most experienced soldiers. The Germans lost many of their idealistic young volunteers.

They called it *Kindermord*, 'The Massacre of the Innocents'. It ended, like most battles on the Western Front, in a costly stalemate.

The Germans made brilliant use of their efficient train network to move troops around the Eastern Front.

Baltic Sea

Masurian Lakes

East Prussia

GERMANY

Tannenberg

RUSSIA

Galicia

Carpathian Mountains

AUSTRIA-HUNGARY

▢ Russian advance

▢ German counter-advance

— front line Dec. 31, 1914

Russian hopes for victory were thwarted early in the War, after two decisive defeats at Tannenberg and the Masurian Lakes.

The Eastern Front

The Germans were right to worry about a war on two fronts. Within a week of the German declaration of war, Russian soldiers had invaded East Prussia. The German High Command saw this as such a threat that they diverted four divisions (100,000 men) designated for the Schlieffen Plan to the East. Like the war in the West, the fighting would result in a bloody, prolonged stalemate. But it took on a different character: the Eastern Front was too big for trench warfare.

Invasion without maps

The Russian invasion of East Prussia was quickly stemmed and the Germans won a stunning victory in August. Two Russian armies were commanded by incompetent rival generals who sent their troops into the marshes and forests of Tannenberg, without maps and with no idea where their enemy was.

The Russians were overpowered by a much smaller German force who made great use of an efficient railway system to ferry troops exactly where they were needed. The second Russian army was annihilated, and its commander, General Samsonov, committed suicide rather than report his loss to the Tsar. A week later, all the Russians in East Prussia were driven out at the Battle of the Masurian Lakes. They wouldn't be able to mount another attack until the following spring.

Austria-Hungary

Russian forces failed against the Germans, but they had some success against Austro-Hungarian soldiers, who were even more badly led and organized than the Russians were.

At the Battle of Galicia, the Russians pushed them back to the Carpathian Mountains. Austro-Hungarian forces also failed to conquer the much smaller Balkan nation of Serbia, which quickly fought off their invasion.

Russian prisoners march into captivity after their crushing defeat at the Masurian Lakes in East Prussia. Boys as young as the prisoner at the front were an unusual sight on most First World War battlefields.

Turkey joins the War

In October, the Central Powers received more good news for their campaign in the East. Turkey joined the war on their side. All at once the eastern Mediterranean became another battleground. The Allies had to stretch their troops and resources to defend another vast area from their enemies.

Ottoman Turkish soldiers were often poorly trained, and just as likely to be fighting the empire's rebellious subjects as the British or French.

God heard the embattled nations sing and shout:

"Gott strafe (punish) England" – "God Save the King"

"God this" – "God that" – and "God the other thing"

"My God," said God, "I've got my work cut out."

A poem by JC Squire 1915

Myths and propaganda

A hundred years ago, people were more likely to believe what they were told by their governments and what they read in newspapers. Many were even convinced that God was 'on their side' and were open to any sign that seemed to prove it.

The angels of Mons

The patriotism and sense of duty felt by the populations of the fighting nations made them vulnerable to propaganda that we would now find absurd. In the late summer of 1914, for example, many British people believed a host of angels came to the aid of exhausted British troops fighting in France. This myth had its roots in a fictional magazine story, which many readers thought was a report of actual events.

This illustration from a magazine of the time shows a host of angels coming to the aid of British troops during the Battle of Mons.

The rape of Belgium

During the German invasion of Belgium, there were executions of 850 civilians, shot in retaliation for attacks by Belgian resistance fighters. Over 1,500 buildings were burned to the ground and hostages were used as 'human shields'.

But this was magnified in the British press into a campaign of mass rape and slaughter. There were bizarre allegations, such as one describing naked nuns being hung from the ropes of church bells. One writer described the invading Germans as 'one vast gang of Jack-the-Rippers' and atrocity stories were reported in lurid detail.

But propaganda, no matter how ridiculous, can have positive results. Tales of German war crimes ensured that many Americans supported the Allies. A totally fictitious story about German 'corpse factories', in which dead soldiers were turned into chemicals, may have helped persuade the Chinese, with their culture of ancestor worship, to join the Allies.

The heroes of Langemarck

Germany was making propaganda too. Many of its best university students had enlisted to fight, and many had been killed in the invasion of Belgium and France.

A myth grew up of these students marching into battle, arm in arm, singing patriotic songs as they were slaughtered in their thousands.

In the 1930s, the Nazis took such stories as truth rather than fiction, and used them as an example of the correct German spirit.

Два друга—колбаснень и его супруга".

REMEMBER BELGIUM

ENLIST TO-DAY

Left: this Russian poster shows the figure of Death looming behind the Kaiser – a clear message to people at home that their country is fighting a murderous, diabolical enemy.

Right: this British poster aimed to remind people of the horrors of the German invasion of Belgium, to encourage them to enlist in the army.

British gun crews lay down a barrage. Although they didn't fight right on the front line, these men were vulnerable to enemy artillery fire.

Artillery shells

There were three main types of artillery shells used in the War.

Standard high explosives, like this one, were designed to make a powerful blast to destroy a building or trench.

Shrapnel was packed with shards of metal or ball bearings. Designed to explode in mid-air, it was very effective against soldiers.

Gas shells released poison gas when they hit the ground, which affected soldiers' eyes and lungs.

A new kind of warfare

The soldiers in the War were unlucky enough to fight at a time when defensive weapons were much better than the weapons of attack. The recent inventions of machine guns and barbed wire, and new kinds of artillery, were daunting obstacles for soldiers armed only with rifles, bayonets and a few grenades. Their commanders had no idea how to develop tactical methods to break this deadlock.

Artillery

Recent advances in military technology had turned artillery into a formidable weapon. Big guns now fired shells packed with powerful new explosives such as dynamite or TNT, as well as shrapnel (shards of metal designed to kill), or gas.

The guns were loaded from the rear, which saved the gunners from having to re-aim every time. During the War, more soldiers were killed by shells than any other kind of weapon.

Machine guns

Perfected in the late 19th century, machine guns were invented by Hiram Maxim, an American based in Britain. Maxim realized that the force of a bullet fired down a barrel, known as the recoil, could be used to eject a spent cartridge and drive a new one into the gun's firing chamber. His machine gun could fire a fearsome 600 bullets a minute and had a devastating effect on attacking infantrymen.

Barbed wire

Barbed wire was invented in 1873 to replace wooden fencing around grazing land for cattle, but it became one of the most effective tools of the War. Difficult to destroy, it proved a deadly hindrance to attacking soldiers under heavy fire. Later in the War, special fuses were developed to destroy it.

"Hang your chemistry and electricity! If you want to make a pile of money, invent something that will enable these Europeans to cut each others' throats with greater facility."

Advice given to Hiram Maxim, inventor of the machine gun, shown above, trying out his invention

This painting, by British war artist Paul Nash, shows a dense web of barbed wire on a Western Front battlefield.

The Christmas Truce

"The Germans opposite us were awfully decent fellows – Saxons, intelligent, respectable-looking men. After our talk I really think a lot of our newspaper reports must be horribly exaggerated."

A British officer in the Westminster rifles, quoted in the *New York Times*, December 30, 1914

The Christmas of 1914 was an especially poignant moment in the War. Soldiers stuck in freezing and muddy trenches must have reflected on the hope that the war would be 'over by Christmas'. Instead, they seemed to be caught in a struggle with no end in sight.

Despite the early propaganda of the War, many ordinary soldiers seem to have felt little real hatred for each other. This became particularly obvious on Christmas Day. On Christmas Eve, German soldiers placed lights on small Christmas trees, in the German tradition, and began singing carols. The trenches of the opposite side were often well within hailing distance, so Allied soldiers must have been able to hear them.

British and German soldiers meet out in No Man's Land at Ploegsteert, Belgium, on Christmas Day 1914.

British and German soldiers meeting up in the
Bridoux-Bancs sector of the Western Front

Christmas spirit

At first light, a few bold soldiers began to peer
out of the trenches – more out of curiosity than
anything. Soon soldiers on either side were
venturing out into No Man's Land (as the gap
between the trenches was known), shaking
hands and talking to their enemies. Some traded
Christmas gifts and even swapped regimental
badges or hats.

Most of the soldiers were British and German.
The French, it seems, felt more hostility towards the
Germans, possibly because of severe French losses
at the start of the War. Also, many of them saw the
War as a chance to take revenge for the humiliation
of the Franco-Prussian War of 1870-71.

This unofficial 'truce' continued until dusk, with
many thousands taking part. When senior officers
on both sides heard about it, they were furious.
Orders were sent down to the trenches that it
should never happen again.

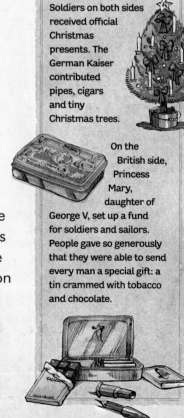

Christmas gifts

Soldiers on both sides
received official
Christmas
presents. The
German Kaiser
contributed
pipes, cigars
and tiny
Christmas trees.

On the
British side,
Princess
Mary,
daughter of
George V, set up a fund
for soldiers and sailors.
People gave so generously
that they were able to send
every man a special gift: a
tin crammed with tobacco
and chocolate.

A German airship and dreadnought battleship are shown here during a navy exercise in 1915.

These expensive advances in technology failed to provide an advantage to either side. German airships introduced a novel form of warfare, though, bombing enemy cities many miles from the front lines. Only in 1916 were fighter planes able to fly high enough to shoot them down.

Chapter 3

1915: Stalemate

As stalemate settled on the Western and Eastern Fronts, military commanders sought new ways to break the deadlock. Looking for their enemy's weak spots, the War spread to the eastern Mediterranean, the Middle East and Africa. The sea lanes between nations became battlegrounds too. The huge numbers of dead had not blunted the appetite for war. Instead, the fighting nations were determined that their fallen soldiers should not die in vain.

Life in the trenches

> "The whole concept of our trench warfare was based on the notion that we, the British, were not stopping in the trenches for long, but were tarrying awhile on the way to Berlin and that soon we would be chasing Jerry across the country."
>
> British veteran
> George Coppard

From late autumn 1914 until spring 1918, the front line on the Western Front moved no more than 16km (10 miles). Trenches were often only 1km (2/3 mile) apart, sometimes as little as 50m (150 ft) or even less.

The German commanders were the first to recognize that the deadlock would be lengthy. So they equipped their trenches better than the Allied ones, with proper living quarters.

The British trenches were especially uncomfortable. Despite the smell of unburied corpses and open latrines, the cold and rain, the lice and the rats that thrived in the filthy conditions, trenches were ideal defensive positions.

Oppy Wood 1917, Evening, by British war artist John Nash, shows the bleak landscape of No Man's Land on a crisp winter evening. Frozen ground was preferable to heavy rain, which turned the trenches into a soggy morass.

As the War dragged on, both sides left deliberate gaps in the barbed wire in front of their trenches, to attract attacking soldiers, so that they could concentrate machine-gun fire on them.

Trench routine

When there was a lull in the fighting, trench life had its own routines. Confined to their underground world, soldiers would clean their weapons and mend passageways and ramparts. Men had to keep their heads down to avoid sniper fire. To peer over the top of the trench invited almost certain death. Some soldiers used mirrors and periscopes, to watch out for enemy attacks.

Despite the discomforts, there were compensations. The postal service to men at the front was so good that food such as cake could be sent from home and still arrive fresh.

When darkness fell, barbed wire could be laid down or repaired and the dead or wounded could be collected from No Man's Land. Sometimes a raiding party was sent over to the enemy trench to capture a soldier for interrogation.

All these activities were highly dangerous. Flares were fired to illuminate the barren ground between the trenches. Any men caught in the open would be quickly despatched with machine-gun fire.

Bitter experience

The future Nazi leader Adolf Hitler served in the trenches as a young man. His bravery won him the Iron Cross, but the experience embittered him and helped to shape his extremist politics. He was photographed on the front line with his pet Jack Russell - dogs were invaluable to soldiers because they hunted the rats that infested their trenches.

Taking leave

Soldiers usually spent a week on a front line trench, then a week in a reserve trench, just behind the front. After that they had two weeks recovering, further behind the line.

Here, some German soldiers are relaxing - playing the piano and preparing food - behind the lines of the Western Front.

Turkey joins the War

In late October 1914, the Turks joined the Central Powers. For the last few hundred years, much of the Middle East had been part of a Turkish power bloc called the Ottoman empire. But, by 1914, Turkey was widely mocked as 'the sick man of Europe'. A lot of former Ottoman territory was in the hands of foreign powers such as Britain. Although nominally ruled by Sultan Mehmed V, Turkey was really run by a group of politicians known as the Young Turks, led by an army officer named Enver Pasha.

The Young Turks

The Turkish armed forces were poorly equipped and badly trained, but the Young Turks aimed to use them to regain control of their empire. This led to direct conflict with the British, who had interests in the area – oil supplies in Mesopotamia (now Iraq), and control of the Suez Canal in Egypt, a vital link between Britain and her empire in India.

The Sultan's jihad

Most Turkish subjects were Muslim. At the urging of the German Kaiser, Sultan Mehmed V had declared *jihad*, or 'holy war', against the Allies. The Kaiser hoped this would lead Muslims in Egypt and India to rise up against the British.

The Ottoman empire in 1914

Germany and Austria-Hungary picked a poor ally in Turkey. The empire, controlled in medieval fashion by a supposedly all-powerful monarch, was a bewildering mixture of languages, religions and racial groups. Some of them were at war with themselves and each other, as well as rebelling against the Ottoman Sultan.

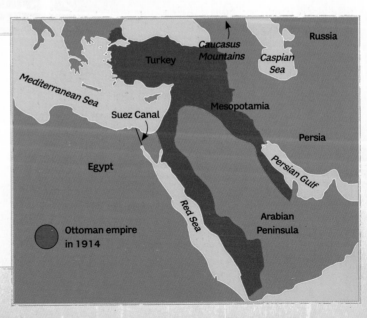

Double disaster

Turkish assaults on Suez and India were fought off by British and Indian troops. Next, the Turks turned their attention to the Caucasus Mountains, an area where the Turks had frequently clashed with the Russians. Poorly prepared troops arrived in time for severe winter weather. When the campaign ground to a halt in early 1915, 30,000 of them had frozen to death and another 45,000 were lost in fighting against hardy Russian troops.

Looking for someone to blame for their defeat, the Turks turned on the Armenians, a local Christian minority. On the pretext of 'holy war', they sent Armenian soldiers to special work camps where they died of exhaustion and disease, and subjected Armenian civilians to a forced march across the Syrian desert. Most of those who survived died in squalid reception camps, or were massacred. Altogether at least 800,000 Armenians perished.

Armenian civilians being marched out of Harput, in Ottoman Turkey, under armed guard, in May 1915

Enver Pasha

Enver Pasha was the power behind the Sultan, but his wartime leadership led to famine, genocide and ruinous inflation. He was exiled after the War, and killed in 1922, fighting with a Central Asian resistance movement against the Bolsheviks.

Gas attack

Dim through the
misty panes and
thick green light,

As under a green
sea, I saw him
drowning.

In all my dreams,
before my helpless
sight,

He plunges at me,
guttering, choking,
drowning.

British officer Wilfred Owen
witnesses a gas attack in his
poem *Dulce et Decorum Est.*

John Singer Sargent's
painting *Gassed* takes its
inspiration from classical
sculptures. But Sargent
makes no attempt to
disguise the ragged
condition and awful plight
of soldiers blinded after a
gas attack.

In late April 1915, French and Canadian soldiers at
Ypres were attacked by a terrifying new weapon. It
wasn't troops or artillery shells, but a great cloud of
yellow chlorine gas. As it burned their throats and
lungs, those that could fled in panic. The attack was
a great success: 6km (4 miles) of the Allied front
line was left temporarily undefended.

The Germans were unprepared for their success.
There weren't enough men available to break
through to the open ground beyond the French
trenches. But gas was obviously effective and it
would be used by both sides for the rest of the war.

It was an especially cruel weapon. Seeping
silently into trenches and dugouts, it caused the
victim's lungs to produce fluid which would drown
him from the inside. Few died immediately, and
most were condemned to a slow, pitiful death in the
field hospitals away from the front.

Progress of sorts

At first, gas was released towards the enemy lines from great steel canisters. But this left the soldiers who deployed it vulnerable if the wind changed direction. A more reliable method was soon employed: by the end of the War 25% of British artillery shells, and up to 80% of German shells, contained gas rather than high explosives.

Chlorine gas dissolves in water, so soldiers facing a gas attack were instructed to wear a damp cloth over their mouths and noses. Gas masks were quickly introduced, both for soldiers and their horses. These offered reliable protection, but made fighting even more miserable and uncomfortable for all sides.

New developments

At first chlorine and phosgene gas was used. This made a soldier vomit and choke and would kill him if he inhaled enough of it.

In September 1917, the Germans began to use the far more deadly mustard gas, which was adopted by the Allies too. This attacked the skin as well as the lungs, causing blindness and terrible blisters.

ANZAC troops (from Australia and New Zealand) recreate an attack for a newspaper photographer, somewhere close to the Turkish front line.

Gallipoli

The harsh landscape of the Gallipoli Peninsula is situated on the edge of the Eastern Mediterranean. Its narrow straits lead to the Sea of Marmara and the Turkish capital, Istanbul, then known as Constantinople.

Gallipoli

As the European powers struggled to break the deadlock, adventurous voices called for a new strategy. In Britain, the First Lord of the Admiralty, Winston Churchill, put forward a plan to attack the Central Powers through their weakest member, Turkey. The plan was bold, but it was deeply flawed.

Churchill hoped the Royal Navy would be able to do most of the fighting. If the Allies could destroy Turkish forces on the Gallipoli Peninsula and Dardanelles Straits, it would be easy for them to reach the Turkish capital, Constantinople. Turkey would have to surrender and Russian warships, trapped in the Black Sea, would be able to attack German and Austro-Hungarian targets in the Mediterranean. But the Dardanelles were heavily defended by mines and forts bristling with artillery.

On March 18, 1915, 16 British and French ships attacked the Straits. Three were immediately sunk by mines and another three were badly damaged.

The troops go in

Only troops on the ground would be able to threaten the Turkish position. On April 25, 52,000 Allied soldiers landed on the Peninsula. They faced a determined enemy who had learned the defensive lessons of the Western Front. Both sides built well-defended trenches and the campaign ground down to a rapid stalemate.

The blazing heat made it a terrible country to fight in. Allied soldiers suffered intense thirst and diseases such as dysentery quickly spread. They were still trying to break the deadlock when winter arrived, bringing frostbite and pneumonia.

This fruitless campaign dragged on for nine months. By the time all the Allied troops had withdrawn in early 1916, they had lost nearly 50,000 men, mostly to disease. But the victors of Gallipoli had fared even worse. The Turks had lost 87,000 soldiers and the fighting strength of their army was exhausted.

The ANZACs

Gallipoli is remembered with particular pride by Australians and New Zealanders. 17,000 of them took part in the fighting, the first major military campaign for both these new nations.

This famous poster tries to make Australian men who stayed at home feel guilty about leaving their friends to do the fighting.

Submarines

During the 19th century, scientific advances enabled shipbuilders to create one of the most successful new weapons of the war: the modern submarine. This tube-like vessel, crammed with machinery and men, used ballast tanks to enable it to sink silently beneath the sea.

Air-guzzling diesel engines propelled it quickly across the surface, while electrical engines were used underwater. Subs were armed with torpedoes – the perfect weapon for an underwater attack.

Both sides used submarines. The most successful was the German *Unterseeboot*, or U-boat. A fleet numbering only 140 U-boats managed to sink nearly 5,000 Allied ships. In 1917 alone, Germany sank 2,439 cargo ships, causing great hardship and severely hindering the British war effort.

The *Lusitania*

U-boats were tremendously effective, but their success also worked against Germany.

In May 1915, *Lusitania*, a famous British liner, was sunk off the coast of Ireland. Among the 1,198 who died were 120 US citizens.

The Germans claimed the ship was carrying munitions, but the sinking turned many neutral Americans against Germany and hastened US entry into the War.

Fighting back

Single cargo vessels were the U-boat commander's most sought-after prey. Submarines often surfaced to sink them with the ship's gun, rather than an expensive torpedo. But this backfired when Allied cargo vessels, known as Q-ships, hid their own guns, only revealing them when the submarine was on the surface.

Devices called hydrophones were invented to pick up the sound of a submarine's electric motors. Once a submarine was located, the ship released high explosive depth charges beneath the waves. They caused fatal damage, or forced the submarine so deep it was crushed by the pressure of the water.

For a cargo ship, the best form of protection was to travel in a convoy: a group of ships, defended by a naval escort. For a U-boat commander, attacking a convoy invited almost certain death.

This German poster from the First World War celebrates the heroism of the U-boat crews, who had a less than 50/50 chance of surviving the War.

A German U-boat braves heavy waters somewhere in the Atlantic. Even in rough seas, the men were always eager to escape the stifling interior for a few moments of air on the conning tower.

French soldiers run towards German front line positions, in this painting by an unknown French artist. Over six million French soldiers were killed or wounded during the War.

Chapter 4

1916: The Big Push

After another year of costly stalemate, and a failed campaign in Gallipoli, generals on all sides wondered what else they could do to break the deadlock. The answer seemed to be bigger battles. Falkenhayn, the German commander in chief, declared his intention to engage the French army and 'bleed them white'. The British military chiefs talked of a 'big push'. They had the men, they had the enormous firepower of 20th century technology. Surely, both sides reasoned, if they applied both in overwhelming numbers, then their enemy would crack.

Eyewitnesses at Verdun

"...what a bloodbath, what horrid images, what a slaughter. Hell cannot be this dreadful. People are insane!"

This diary excerpt of French soldier Alfred Joubaire was his last entry.

"Our poor men have seen too many atrocities... Our poor little mind simply cannot comprehend all of this."

An unidentified German soldier tries to describe the fighting.

The Battle of Verdun

The greatest battle of the War began with a massive bombardment. In the first hour alone, around 1,000 artillery guns fired as many as 100,000 shells. The Germans gave an ominous codename to their attack on the French city of Verdun: *Operation Gericht*. The word had two meanings in German: 'judgement' and 'place of execution'.

The Germans had surrounded the city on three sides. There was no rail link – just a single road exposed to German artillery. Falkenhayn, the German commander, knew French soldiers had been told to hold their ground at all costs. If there wasn't going to be a breakthrough, his soldiers would just have to kill so many Frenchmen that France would be unable to continue fighting.

The campaign began with huge French casualties. The countryside, dotted with stone forts, was turned into a barren lunar landscape.

Long thought to be an actual combat photograph, this shot of French troops fighting and dying at Verdun is from a film recreation of the battle.

The French fight back

But Falkenhayn had underestimated the determination of the French. A new commander, General Philippe Pétain, was determined to hold onto the city. The single shell-peppered route into it, described as the *Voie Sacrée* ('Sacred Road') by French newspapers, was jammed with motor vehicles carrying essential supplies.

French artillery, brought in from all over the Western Front, soon rivalled the Germans in firepower. Most importantly, Pétain constantly rotated his troops, so they would never be too exhausted and demoralized to fight well.

It was the longest, bloodiest battle of the conflict and both sides fought with brutal disregard for the rules. The French suffered 542,000 casualties, the Germans 434,000 – around a third of these may have been actual deaths.

A deadly insight

Pétain recognized that the point of the German attack was to kill as many French soldiers as possible. Capturing ground from the enemy – the usual purpose of a battle – was no longer the point of the fighting.

Although his soldiers were to defend their ground with their lives, they were ordered not to counter-attack.

This French poster commemorates the bravery of the French army at Verdun. The writing behind the ragged French infantryman declares, "They shall not pass!"

Deadly progress

At first, pilots attacked enemy aircraft with pistols, grenades, and even grappling hooks.

Later, machine guns were fitted to the rear or above the wings. This was dangerous as the rear gunner could easily fall out of the plane.

Rear gunner

Then, deflector shields were fitted so the pilot could fire through his propeller without shooting it off. This was also very dangerous.

Finally, Dutch aircraft designer Anthony Fokker invented a mechanism which allowed the gun to fire only when it wouldn't hit the propeller. Pilots could aim their guns by pointing their aircraft at an enemy. The Germans used this system first, but the French and British soon copied it. It made the air war much more dangerous.

Fokker firing mechanism

The air war

In wartime, scientific advances often happen very quickly. In the First World War, this was especially true of aircraft design. In 1914, powered flying machines were wondrous novelties. By 1918, they had added a new dimension to warfare. The sky had become as vital as the ground and the sea.

From spyplane to bomber plane

The first flimsy biplanes of 1914 took to the skies to spot enemy troop movements or artillery positions. But pilots soon encountered enemy planes and a race began to turn their clumsy aircraft into killing machines (see left).

By the end of the war, aircraft were bombing enemy troops in their trenches, as well as enemy cities hundreds of miles behind the front lines. Less than a year later, a British bomber flew across the Atlantic Ocean – a feat unimaginable to the cheering crowds who had welcomed the first plane to fly across the Channel in 1909.

These flimsy fighter planes from the First World War were so dangerous that more pilots died in training than in combat.

Flying battleships

Airships, lifted aloft by lighter-than-air gas such as hydrogen, were also used. At first, they could fly higher and further than ordinary aircraft, and carry a much greater weight in armaments.

The most famous were the zeppelins, named after their German inventor, Count von Zeppelin. These vast airships, the size of ocean liners, terrorized the citizens of enemy cities from London and Paris to Bucharest and Sevastopol.

But their days were numbered once aircraft began to fly higher and faster. Hydrogen gas was also dangerous because it was highly inflammable. It quickly caught fire when attacked by fighter aircraft using incendiary bullets.

Romance of the skies

The exploits of pilots up in the skies seemed romantic, compared to the muddy hell of the trenches.

The most famous pilot of the War was German Baron Manfred von Richthofen (shown below with his dog, Moritz). Known as 'the Red Baron', he shot down over 80 planes and commanded a 'Flying Circus' of first-rate pilots, who painted their aircraft in bright red, blue and yellow.

Women at war

The War had a profound effect on people's lives, and the societies they lived in. For Europeans, especially, the world before and after the War was a strangely different place.

In the years before 1914, many women in Europe and the USA had begun to demand equality with men in areas such as the right to vote and opportunities for work. When men went off to fight, women took over their jobs. It was a chance to prove that women could deliver coal, drive a bus, or work in an office, just as well as men.

Many women took a more direct role in the War, as munitions workers making weapons in factories, or joining the armed forces as 'auxiliaries': cooks, clerks, engineers or dispatch riders. Others took on the harrowing work of nursing the wounded, both close to the battlefield and back at home.

Two famous executions

Edith Cavell, a British nurse, worked in a Belgian Red Cross hospital captured by the Germans. While nursing wounded soldiers, she helped many Allied soldiers escape.

When the Germans found out, she was executed by firing squad. After her death, memorials were built for her in many Allied countries, and streets, hospitals and parks were named after her.

Margaretha Zelle was a beautiful Dutch exotic dancer, known by her stage name of Mata Hari. Before and during the War, she mingled with powerful men on both sides.

Mata Hari was persuaded by both the French and Germans to become a spy. Her luck ran out in 1917, when she was tried and shot for spying by the French.

THESE WOMEN ARE DOING THEIR BIT

LEARN TO MAKE MUNITIONS

As her soldier husband bids a cheery goodbye, the British woman in this poster dons an overall to work in a factory that will supply him with weapons.

Munitions factories could be dangerous, but many women enjoyed the chance to earn an income doing work traditionally performed by men.

Women volunteers train for combat, in St. Petersburg, Russia.

Women on the front line

A few women even fought, something people at the time would have found deeply shocking. In Serbia, around one in four of the population died during the War, and nearly two out of three men who fought were killed. So women joined combat units to make up these losses.

In Russia, many men deserted during the upheavals of the Russian Revolution in 1917. Desperate for troops to continue fighting, the government allowed women volunteers to join their own front line units. They thought this would shame men into fighting.

It didn't work, although the women were reported to have fought bravely. When the War ended, some women also fought in the civil war that followed the Revolution.

Women's land army

This American poster printed in 1918 shows a young woman in her denim overalls working in a field. It calls for women volunteers to work on the land, to allow male agricultural workers to fight in the War.

Get behind *the Girl he left behind him*

Join the land army

The Brusilov Offensive

With France and Germany caught up at Verdun, Russian general, Alexei Brusilov, launched a major assault against Austria-Hungary on the Eastern Front. The Brusilov Offensive, as it became known, was arguably the most successful Russian operation in the entire War. It was also intended to help Italy, who had joined the Allies and was struggling to beat off an Austro-Hungarian attack.

Brusilov

Considered one of the most able generals of the War, Alexei Brusilov was 62 at the time of his greatest campaign, and old enough to have had a grandfather who had fought against Napoleon in 1812.

He became commander in chief of the Russian army in 1917, but lost his command during the Russian Revolution, when he sided with the Bolsheviks (see page 62).

Shock tactics

Much of Brusilov's success was thanks to his imagination. He developed a radical new style of fighting – shock tactics – which caught his opponents by surprise. In June 1916, he attacked the Austro-Hungarians at their weakest spot. His troops dug tunnels out to the enemy lines and used shock troops to stage lightning attacks. Whole divisions – mostly fellow Slavs, who were reluctant citizens of the Austro-Hungarian empire – surrendered to the Russians without a shot.

This map shows the territory fought over by Russian and Austro-Hungarian forces during the *Brusilov Offensive*.

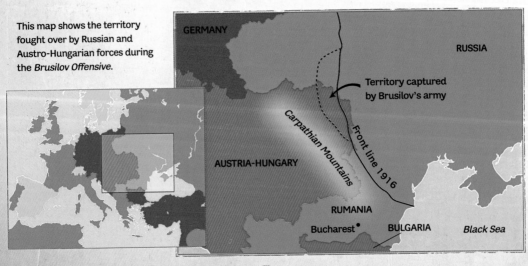

GERMANY

RUSSIA

Territory captured by Brusilov's army

Carpathian Mountains

Front line 1916

AUSTRIA-HUNGARY

RUMANIA

Bucharest •

BULGARIA

Black Sea

A ski unit of an Austro-Hungarian infantry regiment in the Carpathian Mountains prepares to face Brusilov's Russian troops.

By mid-September Brusilov's men had reached the Carpathian Mountains and taken a 100km (60 mile) wide slice of Austro-Hungarian territory (see map). Brusilov also attacked the Germans in the north, but the Germans put up a tough resistance and the attack failed.

Rumania's short war

Encouraged by Brusilov's success in the south, Rumania joined the Allies, but was immediately invaded by Austro-Hungarian, Bulgarian and German forces. Brusilov's attack petered out as his troops were diverted to help. By the end of 1916, the Central Powers had captured the Rumanian capital, Bucharest. Brusilov had succeeded in crushing Austro-Hungarian military strength – but all his gains had been lost and his army was worn out and mutinous. Within a year, Russia would withdraw from the war, torn apart by Revolution.

Rumania

Rumania's King Carol was related to the Kaiser and a strong supporter of the Central Powers, but his subjects were deeply hostile to Austria-Hungary. In the long run, the country did well by siding with the Allies, as they gained considerable Austro-Hungarian territory when the War ended.

RUMANIA'S DAY

THE TWO FORCES

KAISER: "So you, too, are against me! Remember, Hindenburg fights on my side"

KING OF ROUMANIA: "Yes, but freedom and justice fight on mine"

Reproduced by special permission of the Proprietors of "PUNCH"

Blockade

During the War, opposing navies tried to stop or destroy cargo ships sailing to enemy ports. This tactic, known as a 'blockade', was highly effective.

In the Mediterranean and North Seas, the British and French stopped valuable cargos from reaching Germany. The Germans suffered especially during the winter of 1916-17, which became known as 'the turnip winter', after one of the few foodstuffs that was readily available.

But the German and Turkish navies also succeeded in stopping valuable supplies from getting to Russia via the Baltic and Black Seas.

An artist captures the greatest sea battle of the War, as British and German warships clash at Jutland.

The Battle of Jutland

In 1916, Britain and Germany had the two most powerful navies in the world. After two years of small raids in the North Sea, the two fleets finally met head-on off the coast of Jutland, in Denmark. But, after the largest steel ship battle ever seen, both sides claimed victory.

Led by admirals John Jellicoe and Reinhard Sheer, it was said that either 'could lose the War in an afternoon'. A massive defeat would enable the winner to cut off all sea trade to the enemy. For example, if the German navy dominated English coastal waters, it would make transporting men and supplies to France extremely dangerous, and almost impossible to supply Britain with food.

Despite the risks, Sheer decided to sail his High Seas Fleet from his base at Wilhelmshaven in North Germany, to head for hostile waters. He planned to lure the British Grand Fleet from its moorings on the east coast of Scotland – and to destroy it.

Time for action

The British picked up German radio messages and knew their enemy had taken to sea. On May 31, a squadron under Admiral David Beatty set out to intercept them. He engaged with the German fleet and swiftly lost two of his ships. So he turned tail, intending to lead the German fleet towards a much larger British one to the North.

The two fleets clashed at the Battle of Jutland. Although German guns were superior, Sheer decided he was dangerously outnumbered. His fleet retreated under cover of smoke.

Winners and losers

The battle had been short and swift. The Germans had sunk more British ships and killed more British sailors. But Jellicoe had sent the German fleet back to port, where it remained for the rest of the War. The British still ruled the North Sea and kept total control over the vital English Channel.

John Cornwell

John 'Jack' Cornwell was a delivery boy who ran away to sea at 15. In 1916, aged 16, he was mortally wounded at the Battle of Jutland. He was given the Victoria Cross, Britain's highest award for bravery, for remaining at a gun on *HMS Chester* when all around him were killed.

Following his death from wounds, he became famous throughout the British Commonwealth. Streets, pubs, hospital wards, Sea Scout bases in Australia, a mountain in Canada, and even a Boy Scout medal, were all named after him.

Pals battalions

In Britain, posters like this, featuring Minister of War Lord Kitchener, inspired many young men to volunteer – often joining 'Pals Battalions', where they could fight alongside friends from the same town. It was a disastrous idea: when casualties were heavy, a town could lose many of its young men in a single day.

The Somme

July 1, 1916, the first day of the Battle of the Somme, has become the most infamous day in British military history. The commander in chief who masterminded it, Lord Haig, was so convinced God was on his side that he said, "I feel every step of my plan has been taken with the Divine help."

It was to be the first experience of battle for hundreds of thousands of men who had volunteered to fight at the start of the War. Like Verdun, the battle began with a massive artillery attack. British troops were told the week-long bombardment, using 1,500,000 shells, would destroy the German front line and make any survivors too dazed to fight. But the Germans had prepared their fortifications well.

BRITONS

"WANTS" YOU

JOIN YOUR COUNTRY'S ARMY!

GOD SAVE THE KING

Reproduced by permission of LONDON OPINION

Most escaped, shaken but uninjured, sheltering in dugouts 10m (30 ft) below ground. The barbed wire in front of their trenches was blown into the air by shellfire, but settled again, still intact.

When the artillery barrage lifted at 7:30 that morning, the Germans scrambled back up to their trench parapets and set up their guns. Advancing British troops suffered heavy casualties. On that first morning, 20,000 men were killed and 40,000 injured. Most died in the first hour or so.

The British advance, over a 40km (25 mile) front, achieved no lasting breakthrough. But the battle still went on until November, when winter weather brought it to a halt. By then, the Battle of the Somme had claimed over a million lives.

Faulty tactics

Many British troops went into action carrying 32kg (70lbs) of equipment.

They were also told to keep going forward in neat columns. Haig thought his men were too inexperienced to do anything else.

British or Commonwealth troops negotiate a path through a landscape destroyed by war, in November 1916. This was what remained of the Ancre Valley on the Somme, after four months of fighting.

Italian troops advance across the roof of the Alps in a bloody but almost forgotten battlefield of the War.

The War in Africa

At the start of the War, Britain and France controlled much of Africa. Germany had few colonies there, but turned out to be a tenacious foe. German East Africa (now Tanzania) was cut off from supplies and reinforcements, but Colonel von Lettow-Vorbeck (see below) controlled a small German force who fought a campaign against the British for the entire War.

A global war

While most of the heaviest fighting took place on the Western and Eastern Fronts and Gallipoli, other areas of the world were also scarred by the War.

Mountain fighting

The Italians were technically allied to Germany and Austria-Hungary, but proved to be fickle friends. Initially refusing to join the War, they sided with the Allies in April 1915, hoping to gain territory on their northern border from Austria-Hungary.

But the terrain of the high Alps was one of the toughest battlegrounds of the entire War. Troops suffered from altitude sickness and frostbite, as they fought on rock faces and glaciers. Tens of thousands were swept away by avalanches. Altogether, 650,000 soldiers died in this barely remembered corner of the War.

Desert war

One of the most important areas of the War was the Middle East – significant, just as now, because it produced oil, essential for all the nations at war.

In 1914, this area was mainly controlled by the empire of the Ottoman Turks. So the British tried to enlist the help of their disaffected Arab subjects. T.E. Lawrence, a charismatic young British officer who spoke Arabic and had a deep interest in the history of the area, persuaded powerful Arab tribal leaders to support the British. He helped lead a guerrilla force that disrupted Turkish supplies and communications.

Lawrence's fighters helped the British to seize important territories and oil supplies. The British Egyptian Expeditionary Force commanded by General Edmund Allenby won significant victories, capturing Jerusalem in December 1917, and Megiddo in September 1918 – a breakthrough that led the Turks to sue for peace in October 1918.

Lawrence became popularly known as 'Lawrence of Arabia'. The British public saw him as a very romantic figure, not least because of the Arab robes and headgear he wore to help him cope with the desert heat.

Conflict in the Far East

Japan joined the War to fight with the Allies. In September 1914, 50,000 Japanese soldiers, with a smaller Anglo-Indian force, attacked a German naval base at Tsingtao on the Chinese coast. The Germans defended their base with 3,000 marines, holding out for two months before they surrendered.

The Battle of Tsingtao painted by a Japanese war artist in traditional style

This shot by Frank Hurley of the devastated and waterlogged landscape of the battlefield near Passchendaele became one of the most famous photographs of the War.

Chapter 5

1917: Cracks and catastrophes

After three years, the warring sides fought on, but cracks were beginning to show. Hindenburg and Ludendorff took over as joint German commanders and the country became a military dictatorship. In the East, the exhausted armies of the Tsar refused to continue and Russia surrendered. In the West, half the French army mutinied. The USA had decided to join the Allies but it was now a race against time. With only one front to fight on, the Germans could unleash their military might. But would they be able to do so before the Americans arrived?

The Russian Revolution

Russia was the largest and most populated country on the Allied side, but it was also the weakest, politically and industrially well behind Britain, France, Germany and the USA. Russia's Tsar Nicholas II believed he had a God-given right to rule his sprawling empire, but he was unsuited to the role that history had thrust upon him.

Before the War, Nicholas had already faced open revolt in 1905. Three years into the conflict, his people were exhausted and starving. In March 1917, soldiers in St. Petersburg joined forces with rioters protesting against the War. Nicholas abdicated, and a new government was set up under Alexander Kerensky. Kerensky's government was determined to continue the War and this was their undoing. A summer offensive, led by General Brusilov, turned into a disastrous retreat.

Nicholas, shown here with his ill-fated family, was not as dull as he is sometimes portrayed. He spoke three foreign languages, including English, which he spoke to his German wife, Alexandra, a granddaughter of Queen Victoria's.

Soviet propaganda turned the storming of the Winter Palace into a heroic epic. Paintings like this helped to stoke this myth.

This Soviet poster from the Revolutionary era proclaims, "Long Live the Socialist Revolution!" and features Lenin making a dramatic speech.

New rulers

As Russia's armies collapsed, another political party was waiting in the wings. Led by Vladimir Ilyich Ulyanov, known as Lenin, the Bolsheviks promised 'Peace, Bread and Land' and a completely new society. They planned to end the War, seize farm land from the aristocracy to give to the peasants, and give industrial workers control of the factories. This new system of government, based on the ideas of Karl Marx and Friedrich Engels, became known as communism.

In October 1917, with the country on the brink of anarchy, Bolsheviks occupied the Winter Palace, home of Kerensky's government, declaring themselves Russia's new rulers. Hardly a shot was fired and only six Bolshevik soldiers were killed. Nicholas and his family were murdered in 1918, and Russia was plunged into a bloody civil war. By 1922, the Bolsheviks were in control of the country, which was renamed the Soviet Union (after *soviet*, the word for a council).

Russia's disastrous peace

In March 1918, the Bolshevik leaders withdrew from the War and made peace with the Germans at Brest-Litovsk (shown here).

They gave up much of western Russia – containing a third of their population, half their industry and most of their coal. But they believed there would be further communist revolutions in Europe and that the new nations would return their land and resources to them.

Mutinies and rebellions

The Easter Rising

At Easter, 1916, rebels calling themselves the Irish Citizen Army, and demanding independence from Britain, seized the city of Dublin. The uprising was swiftly crushed and rebel leaders were shot. They had had little support among the Irish people, but their executions prompted outrage. This spurred the south of the country to a successful war of independence, as soon as the Great War had ended.

For the French, Verdun had been a victory of sorts. The city had not fallen, but the battle had broken the spirit of the army. The commander in chief, Robert Nivelle, launched another offensive in April 1917, at Chemin des Dames, claiming it would end the War in 48 hours. But it resulted in 180,000 casualties. It was the final straw.

That month, French troops showed their contempt for their leaders by marching to battle bleating like sheep to be slaughtered. In May, whole divisions refused to fight. Some even threatened to march on Paris and depose France's rulers. By June, 54 divisions – half the French army – were in a state of open rebellion. Now no reliable troops stood between the front line and Paris.

Irish rebels pose for pictures during the Easter Rising, 1916. Their slogan was, 'Neither King nor Kaiser but Ireland' – a plain-speaking declaration to avoid accusations of betraying their country.

Exhausted and demoralized French
troops, around the time of the mutiny

The French mutiny could have handed the
Germans victory on a plate. But the Germans
knew nothing about it. The French government was
making frantic efforts to keep it secret and restore
order behind the lines. Nivelle was replaced in May
1917 by Philippe Pétain, the hero of Verdun. The
mutineers were punished and the 'ringleaders' were
executed. Others, condemned to death, had their
sentences commuted to exile in the notorious prison
colony of French Guiana. A Russian division, sent
as a gesture of friendship, had mutinied too. They
were surrounded by artillery and shot.

But there were carrots as well as sticks. Pétain
provided his demoralized soldiers with more leave
and better food. He promised no more major
offensives until US soldiers, and the new tanks,
arrived in overwhelming numbers.

Home on leave

French army command was
wise enough to realize that
exhausted men needed
to be taken better care
of. After the revolt, the
poilu (ordinary soldier)
was given more time away
from the front - something
commemorated in a series
of prints, like the one above,
produced towards the end
of the War.

Woodrow Wilson

Many American citizens wanted to have nothing to do with the War. US President Woodrow Wilson won his 1916 election campaign with the slogan, "He kept us out of the War!"

The USA enters the War

Across the Atlantic, the citizens of the USA watched the War with dismay. Among recent immigrants from Europe, feelings were divided, as many had German ancestry. Others simply felt they'd had a lucky escape. Yet in 1917 the USA joined the Allies against the Central Powers.

The Zimmerman telegram

The year 1917 started badly for Germany. Fearing that the USA was a natural ally of Britain's, the foreign secretary, Arthur Zimmerman, promised to help Mexico regain its former territories of Texas, New Mexico and Arizona if they would join the Central Powers in the event of war. Zimmerman's coded telegram was intercepted and deciphered by the British who promptly showed it to the Americans. The news caused predictable outrage, especially as relations between the USA and Mexico were often hostile.

Posters like these were produced by the US government to drum up support for the War.

U-boat gamble

Then, in February, German commander in chief Ludendorff took a desperate gamble. Previously, German submarines had only had orders to attack Allied ships. Now Ludendorff gave them permission to attack any ship sailing to Allied ports. This meant US cargo and passenger ships became targets too. The Germans knew this was likely to result in the US joining the War. But they hoped to starve Britain into defeat before US troops arrived in Europe.

They almost succeeded. Between February and April, over a thousand merchant ships were sunk. Britain was four weeks away from running out of essential supplies. But, due to the introduction of convoys, the U-boats couldn't sink enough ships to make a crucial difference.

As expected, President Wilson declared war on Germany on April 6, 1917, stating his intention to 'make the world safe for democracy' and protect shipping lanes for international trade.

American troops, many of whom will never have been away from home before, put on a display of excitement and enthusiasm for the newspapers, as their troop ship prepares to leave New York.

Flexing muscles

The United States entered the War with an army of 100,000 men and an air service of 35 pilots. They immediately put all their energy and enthusiasm into building up their armed forces.

TOGETHER WE WIN
UNITED STATES SHIPPING BOARD ——— EMERGENCY FLEET CORPORATION

By the time the War ended a year and a half later, there were 3.5 million US soldiers in Europe, and the US Army Air Service had 45 squadrons operating over the Western Front.

Tanks

Tanks, one of the most important weapons of the 20th century, had never been used before the outbreak of the First World War. The idea of a 'land battleship' or 'mobile fortress' had been the dream of military planners for centuries. But the new demands of trench warfare finally led the dream to become reality.

Why 'tanks'?

The British called their mobile fortresses 'tanks' as a ruse to hide their true purpose. They wanted the Germans to think these mechanical monsters were mobile water tanks.

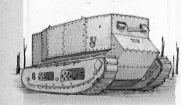

The first battle tanks

The earliest tanks were developed by the British, who used them for the first time at Flers, during the Battle of the Somme in September 1916. They were slow and unreliable and look clumsy to us now. Out of 49 tanks, over 30 broke down or got stuck on their journey to their start positions.

A squadron of British tanks advances across open territory, towards the end of the War.

But they could be tremendously effective on the battlefield. The few that reached the German trenches caused absolute mayhem. The sound of these clunking metal-plated monsters, spitting fire from machine guns and cannons, terrified the German soldiers, who fled before them. Their caterpillar tracks crushed barbed wire and their metal casing was impervious to the machine-gun fire that had proved so lethal to attacking infantry.

British tanks were used again at Cambrai in November 1917. In a single day, 476 of them spearheaded an advance of 12km (7.5 miles) into enemy territory. At the 3rd Battle of Ypres, between July and November, the Allies had gained a similar distance with the loss of nearly 250,000 men.

In the belly of the beast

The first tanks were fiendishly difficult to operate. Inside, men were deafened by the noise of the engine and of their own guns. The tank commander had to communicate with his crew by banging a wrench on the metal engine frame.

Poor ventilation made it hot and airless, too. Crews wore chainmail visors to protect their eyes from molten shards that flew around when shells and bullets hit the outside.

The wooden structures on the front of the tanks were intended to help them cross enemy trenches or other obstacles dug into the ground.

Paul Nash's painting '*The Menin Road*' captures the devastation of the 3rd Battle of Ypres.

"There was not a sign of life of any sort. Not a tree, save for a few dead stumps which looked strange in the moonlight. Not a bird, not even a rat or a blade of grass. Nature was as dead as those Canadians whose bodies remained where they had fallen the previous autumn. Death was written large everywhere."

Private R.A. Colwell describes the landscape around Passchendaele, two months after the battle.

Haig's disastrous plan

The year 1917 began well for British and Commonwealth troops on the Western Front. There were small-scale successes at Arras, Vimy Ridge and Messines. Commander in chief Douglas Haig hoped it was a sign the Germans were exhausted, and he became more ambitious, planning a knockout blow to demolish the German army.

In the Flanders region, which had already been the site of heavy fighting, both the British and the Germans had dense communications networks close to the front lines. Haig reasoned that a breakthrough here of only 10 or 20 km (7 or 14 miles) would throw the enemy into severe disorder.

Once again, he was planning a battle that could win the War. The fact that German U-boat bases lay close by on the occupied Belgian coast made the prospect of victory even more tempting.

The 3rd Battle of Ypres

The campaign that began on July 31 became known as 'the 3rd Battle of Ypres'. The infantry waited ten days while British artillery pounded German positions. But instead of destroying the enemy, the bombardment turned the marshy plain into a muddy quagmire. Drainage systems were destroyed, and there was the worst summer rain for 30 years.

A sea of mud

When the Allies attacked, tens of thousands vanished into the mud. Directing the battle miles behind the front line, High Command didn't appreciate the appalling conditions in the field.

The battle ended on November 6: a few small gains had been made, at the cost of nearly 250,000 British casualties.

Haig's new idea

Haig's plan was opposed by the prime minister, who wanted to wait for US troops before another major offensive. But Haig believed his tactic would prevent huge losses.

A 'creeping barrage' of artillery fire would be laid down in front of advancing troops, to prevent the enemy from firing at them. But such tactics could prove fatal to the attackers – especially when assaults didn't go according to plan.

Canadian generals, painted by Sir William Nicholson, in front of a photograph of the ruined city of Ypres. The battle came to a climax with the capture of the town of Passchendaele by Canadian troops.

When Germany surrendered on November 11, 1918, the country was already on the brink of anarchy. Revolutionary soldiers and sailors are pictured in Berlin two days earlier, inciting civilians to take part in a communist revolution to end the War and depose their discredited rulers.

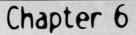

Chapter 6

Collapse

With the war in Russia over, the victorious German army began to transfer a million men over to the Western Front. Their strategy: to destroy the French and British armies before fresh American troops arrived in strength. Now, after over three years of all-out war and unimaginable carnage, the European nations were reeling. It was impossible to predict who would topple first, and once again the generals called upon their exhausted troops to stand fast and fight hard.

Germany unleashed

The Germans faced the new year with renewed strength. With the Russians out of the War, they were free from the two-front war that had divided their resources. They now prepared to destroy their enemies in the West.

As well as a million extra men from the East, German military leaders had new tactics to break the three-year trench deadlock. A new kind of soldier – the stormtrooper – would be the key to victory (see left). As winter receded, the German army launched a final great assault in March 1918, which became known as 'the Spring Offensive'.

Stormtrooper assault

Stormtrooper attacks began with an artillery bombardment, but this time it was more intense and accurate.

Small groups of highly trained stormtroopers probed the Allied front line bypassing strongly defended positions and searching for weak spots. When they found them, they attacked with flame-throwers, grenades and machine guns.

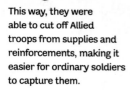

This way, they were able to cut off Allied troops from supplies and reinforcements, making it easier for ordinary soldiers to capture them.

German stormtroopers rehearsing assault tactics in preparation for the Spring Offensive of 1918

Allied collapse

In March, a German attack against British forces at St. Quentin was a great success. Recognizing the huge danger his forces were in, British commander Douglas Haig requested that one commander in chief should control all Allied forces. French General Ferdinand Foch took on this role.

In April, the Germans struck another powerful blow. Fearing defeat, Haig issued orders to British troops, declaring, "With our backs to the wall… each one of us must fight to the end." His soldiers held on with grim determination and, this time, the British line buckled but did not break.

German Commander Ludendorff searched for further weak spots. In May and June, his troops advanced towards Paris, causing panic in the city. When they reached the Marne, Allied forces hit back, reinforced by fresh US troops. Once again the German advance ground to a halt.

Ludendorff's folly

Intoxicated by victory in the East, Ludendorff kept many of his troops on Russian territory, intent on adding the Crimea and the Don Basin to land the Germans had already seized.

If these extra troops had been deployed in the West during the Spring Offensive, the Germans might have achieved their breakthrough.

The Doughboys

US troops sent to Europe, known as the American Expeditionary Force, were greeted with scepticism by the British and French, who wondered if they would have the will and training to fight.

Nicknamed 'Doughboys' – because of their plump, well-fed faces or generous pay – these inexperienced soldiers proved determined fighters. In this final stage of the War, the US army lost 126,000 troops, with another 250,000 wounded.

The final breakthrough

In spring 1918, as the German army ran itself into the ground, hundreds of thousands of US soldiers were arriving in France. The Allies fought back with renewed strength. Not only did they have fresh troops, they were now equipped with hundreds of tanks. These lumbering mobile fortresses proved immensely effective in the months ahead.

A successful French counter-attack on the Marne began the final push to victory. In June and July, the Allies moved slowly east. On August 8, British and Australian troops and tanks broke through German lines at Amiens. For the first time in the War, German commanders faced defeat. Ludendorff called it 'a black day for the German army'. Order was restored, but there was no longer any hope of a German victory.

War artist Will Longstaff depicts Australian soldiers, accompanied by tanks, breaking through the German Hindenburg Line. The destruction of this powerful defensive position marked the beginning of the end for the German army.

Trouble at home

Although the German army continued an orderly retreat, there was greater trouble inside Germany itself. The British naval blockade had denied them food and essential supplies throughout the War. The population was weak with hunger and arms manufacturers starved of materials. The Germans had never been able to develop tanks to match the Allies, because they didn't have enough steel.

Although they knew there was no chance of victory, Germany's leaders still hoped for a peace settlement that would leave them undefeated. The Kaiser, too, refused to step down. German soldiers continued to die and civilians continued to starve. The threat of a revolution, like the one that had toppled the Tsar in Russia, hung in the air.

Allied breakthroughs

This map shows the location of Allied breakthroughs at the en d of the War.

North Sea

BELGIUM

Ypres

Cambrai

Somme

Hindenburg Line

Amiens

FRANCE

Belleau Wood

Paris

Second Marne

✳ Battle
✦ Breakthrough battles

The war ends

As their troops fell back to their own borders, Germany's allies faced their own catastrophes. The Turks, who had ruled most of the Middle East for 400 years, were too weak to fight on.

In Eastern Europe, Bulgarian troops fled from Allied forces who attacked their border from Salonika in Greece. The Austro-Hungarian empire was disintegrating from within. There were crippling food shortages and rebellious national groups began to call for independence.

For Germany, the final collapse came from within its own borders. The High Seas Fleet was ordered to take on the Royal Navy in a fight to the death. The sailors mutinied and refused to go, and there were riots in the street.

The fatal last day

News that the War had ended filtered out to front line troops over the morning. But many commanders pressed on with planned attacks, hoping to gain last minute glory and further advantage over the undefeated Germans.

Artillery bombardments continued on all sides until the final moments, and men still died later in the day from unexploded shells, booby traps and misunderstandings.

A sailor from the German navy waves a communist red flag during a demonstration against the War in Berlin, on November 9, 1918. He is joined by civilians and soldiers on leave from the Front.

Many soldiers had picked up communist ideas from the Russians on the Eastern Front and Germany was on the brink of a revolution. A new government was formed to try to end the War.

But the Allies refused to negotiate while the Kaiser was still in power, so Wilhelm II took a train to exile in the Netherlands.

British and French delegates photographed outside the railway carriage at Compiègne, where the ceasefire was signed.

Negotiations begin

Representatives from German political parties and the armed forces travelled to Compiègne forest, 100 km (60 miles) behind the Allied lines. They met on the private train of Marshal Foch, the Supreme Commander of the Allied Armies.

The ceasefire

On November 11, 1918, at 5:10, an armistice – an agreement to stop fighting – was finally signed. It would take six hours to come into effect, so the representatives agreed to say they had signed at 5:00. The War finished at 11:00, with heavy fighting right up to the final moments.

The Allies did not trust their defeated enemy. So they threatened to start fighting again within 48 hours if any of the peace terms was broken.

One of the last men to die?

One story tells of a German officer, Lieutenant Tomas, who approached American soldiers on the Meuse-Argonne sector of the Western Front, to tell them his men were leaving houses they had occupied in a nearby village. Although it was after 11:00, these American soldiers did not know about the ceasefire, and shot him dead.

A war widow hurries from Buckingham Palace in London, after receiving a medal awarded to her dead husband. Widows were the forgotten victims of the conflict, along with hundreds of thousands of women on all sides unable to marry or have children because of the great shortage of young men after the War.

Chapter 7

1919: The flawed peace

The conflict had been so terrible it was described as 'the war to end all war'. The peace treaties that followed tried to ensure the combatant nations would never fight again. But bad judgement and ill will ensured another war would be inevitable.

Many people, including the British prime minister David Lloyd George, knew this at the time. He confided to a colleague: "We shall have to do the same thing again in 25 years and at three times the cost."

He was broadly right. The Second World War broke out 20 years later, and cost four times as many lives.

Peace at Versailles

Peace negotiations began at the French palace of Versailles, outside Paris. The three main victors, Britain, France and the USA, all wanted to prevent Germany from starting another war. But they had very different ideas about how to do this.

France's elderly prime minister, Georges Clemenceau, had seen the industrial northeast of his country reduced to ruins. Half of all Frenchmen between 20 and 35 had been killed or wounded in the War. Clemenceau wanted a treaty that would make it impossible for Germany to wage war again and he was not inclined to be generous.

A chance of reconciliation

On the other hand, US President Woodrow Wilson wanted a settlement with Germany which would offer the chance of reconciliation. But he lacked the political skills to achieve his ideas. He had already annoyed his Allies by announcing '14 points', or policies, for the postwar world.

They included a League of Nations for countries to discuss their differences, and a recognition of the 'rights of all people to self-determination' – to be free of control by other countries. But the British and French had no intention of giving independence to their own colonies.

Make Germany pay

These were the terms of the Peace of Versailles:

- Germany would have to pay 50 billion German marks as 'reparations' to France and Britain for starting the War. The sum was so vast it would take nearly 100 years to pay.

- The German armed forces would be greatly reduced, making it impossible for them to attack other countries.

- German overseas colonies would be given to Britain and France.

- The Germans lost not only all their First World War conquests in Europe, but some lands they had obtained before the War, notably in the East.

Map showing boundary changes following the Treaty of Versailles

North Sea

Baltic Sea

Memel

Eupen-Mamedy

GERMANY

Poznania

Allenstein
Marienwerder

Rhine

Saar Rhineland

Western
Upper Silesia

Eastern
Upper Silesia

Alsace-Lorraine

○ Land held by Germany   ○ Land lost by Germany

○ Land held after vote   ○ Land held but
by local population   demilitarized zone

Stuck in the middle

The British prime minister, David Lloyd George, saw the sense in Wilson's arguments, but he had an election to win. After four years of war, with nearly a million dead, British voters were in no mood for reconciliation. 'Make Germany Pay' and 'Hang the Kaiser' were popular slogans of the time. So in public he sided with Clemenceau, but behind the scenes he tried to get people to listen to Wilson.

The Germans were not invited to take part – something they regarded as a harsh insult. Instead, they were summoned to sign the treaty on June 28, 1919, the same day Archduke Franz Ferdinand had been shot five years before. The world had changed in a way no one could have imagined. The Germans were outraged by the terms, but they had no choice: the British naval blockade was still in place and the German people were still starving.

Uncanny prediction

This cartoon in the *Daily Herald* about the Versailles treaty predicted the future with uncanny accuracy.

PEACE AND FUTURE CANNON FODDER

The Tiger: "Curious! I seem to hear a child weeping!"

"Curious! I seem to hear a child weeping!" it says, predicting another war by 1940.

The peace settlement was signed in the dazzling setting of the Hall of Mirrors at the Palace of Versailles.

Redrawing the map

The Treaty of Versailles was only one of several agreements to redraw the map after the War. In other settlements, German allies, Austria-Hungary, Bulgaria and the Ottoman Turks, also lost territory.

The Austro-Hungarian empire was broken up and new nations created, but the new borders were ill thought out. New countries based around specific ethnic groups often included minorities who spoke different languages or followed different religions. These new borders became the cause of wars for the rest of the century.

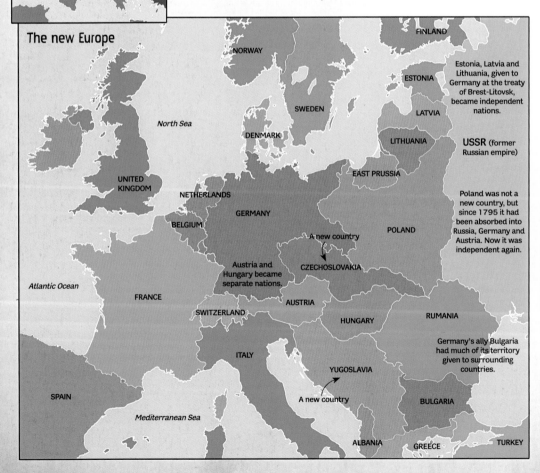

Eastern Europe in 1914

GERMANY
RUSSIA
AUSTRIA
ITALY
BOSNIA
SERBIA
RUMANIA
BULGARIA
MONTENEGRO
ALBANIA
TURKEY
GREECE

The new Europe

FINLAND
NORWAY
ESTONIA
SWEDEN
LATVIA
North Sea
DENMARK
LITHUANIA
EAST PRUSSIA
UNITED KINGDOM
NETHERLANDS
GERMANY
BELGIUM
POLAND
A new country
Austria and Hungary became separate nations.
CZECHOSLOVAKIA
Atlantic Ocean
FRANCE
AUSTRIA
SWITZERLAND
HUNGARY
RUMANIA
ITALY
YUGOSLAVIA
SPAIN
A new country
BULGARIA
Mediterranean Sea
ALBANIA
GREECE
TURKEY

Estonia, Latvia and Lithuania, given to Germany at the treaty of Brest-Litovsk, became independent nations.

USSR (former Russian empire)

Poland was not a new country, but since 1795 it had been absorbed into Russia, Germany and Austria. Now it was independent again.

Germany's ally Bulgaria had much of its territory given to surrounding countries.

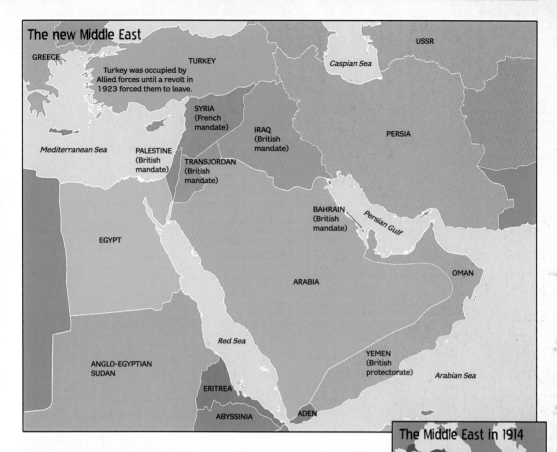

The new Middle East

GREECE

TURKEY

Turkey was occupied by
Allied forces until a revolt in
1923 forced them to leave.

Caspian Sea

USSR

SYRIA
(French
mandate)

IRAQ
(British
mandate)

PERSIA

Mediterranean Sea

PALESTINE
(British
mandate)

TRANSJORDAN
(British
mandate)

BAHRAIN
(British
mandate)

Persian Gulf

EGYPT

ARABIA

OMAN

Red Sea

ANGLO-EGYPTIAN
SUDAN

YEMEN
(British
protectorate)

Arabian Sea

ERITREA

ABYSSINIA

ADEN

The Middle East in 1914

TURKISH
OTTOMAN EMPIRE

PERSIA

EGYPT

ARABIAN
PENINSULA

The Middle East

The postwar settlement in the Middle East had long
term consequences. In exchange for support, the
British had promised Arab leaders independence
from their Turkish rulers. But these promises were
broken. Instead, the British and French were given
control of Arab lands, known as a mandate, and
set about exploiting resources, particularly oil.

In the Balfour Declaration of 1917, the British
declared sympathy for a Jewish homeland in
Palestine – a step towards the creation of the state
of Israel. The arrival of Jewish settlers led to conflict
with local Muslim inhabitants, which has caused
upheaval and warfare in the Middle East ever since.

Remembering the War

A century on from its beginning, the First World War still haunts our imagination. Books, films and television dramas continue to draw in millions of viewers and readers, ensuring the War remains fresh in people's memories.

War literature

Among the greatest works of literature produced after the War are *Goodbye To All That* by Robert Graves, *Testament of Youth* by Vera Brittain, *All Quiet on the Western Front* by Erich Maria Remarque, and *A Farewell to Arms* by Ernest Hemingway. Poetry also found a lasting audience, notably in the works of British poets such as Siegfried Sassoon and Wilfred Owen, whose work is still widely studied in the English-speaking world.

You smug-faced crowds with kindling eye

Who cheer when soldier lads march by,

Sneak home and pray you'll never know

The hell where youth and laughter go.

Siegfried Sassoon
'Suicide in the Trenches'

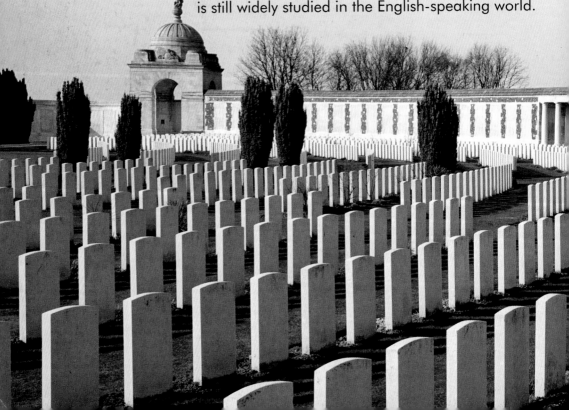

Painting the War

The War also inspired great works of art – from the heroic, formal *Gassed* by John Singer Sargent (see pages 38-39) to works by war artists John and Paul Nash (see pages 29 and 34), to Otto Dix's grotesque *War Cripples*, shown here.

German artist Otto Dix fought in the War and had recurring nightmares for the rest of his life. The Nazis hated his work so much they burned much of it, including this painting here.

War memorials

The most permanent reminders of the War are probably the thousands of monuments and memorials to commemorate the dead and missing, scattered throughout the towns and villages of Europe, the countries of the former British empire and the battlefields of the Western Front.

Over 10,000 British and Commonwealth soldiers lie buried here, at Tyne Cot Cemetery, close to the location of the 3rd Battle of Ypres. These men were all killed between 1917 and 1918.

The Great War and the 20th century

Apart from the disastrous consequences of the postwar peace treaties in the Balkans and Middle East, the War had a deep and lasting influence on many other aspects of life in the 20th century.

Empires in decline

Britain and France had used up so much of their wealth fighting the War, that they were now shadows of the world powers they used to be. The colonies they had fought to preserve began demanding independence.

Mahatma Gandhi, who led India to independence after the Second World War.

The German dictator Adolf Hitler giving a speech to his Nazi Party followers

Germany's return

Defeat came as a terrible shock to many Germans and the peace treaty added hugely to their resentment. When Hitler blamed Jews and communists and promised to make his country great again, he found many enthusiastic supporters, making the Second World War inevitable.

The Soviet experiment

In Russia, the War ended with revolution. The new communist leaders provided better education and healthcare, and created a powerful industrial nation, but they inflicted famine, repression and mass murder on their people.

Soviet dictator Joseph Stalin built Russia into a powerful industrial nation at a terrible human cost.

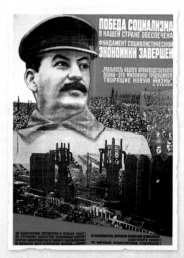

USA rises to the top

In 1918, the USA emerged as the richest, most powerful country in the world. US industry manufactured goods that would change people's lives: radios, refrigerators, washing machines, vacuum cleaners and motor cars. US culture, in the form of Jazz music and Hollywood films, became popular throughout the world.

Fashionable American girls dance along the edge of a 'skyscraper'.

Women's lives

With so many war dead, millions of women were left to grow old alone. But they had proved their worth in the face of old prejudices in difficult wartime jobs. As the century rolled on, most countries gave women the vote, and women began to take up positions in work and politics unimaginable in 1914.

A woman casts her vote for the first time in an election.

The end of deference

The War also chipped away at authority, as ordinary people no longer assumed their social superiors were better able to run the country than themselves. Soldiers returning from the trenches expected some reward.

British workers march to London demanding work. Many of these men are former soldiers who felt betrayed by their government.

Timeline of the First World War

Here are the major events in the story of the First World War.

June 1914

Austria's Archduke Franz Ferdinand assassinated in Sarajevo by Serbian anarchist Gavrilo Princip.

July 1914

Austria-Hungary declares war on Serbia.

Russia begins to mobilize troops to defend Serbian allies.

August 1914

Austria-Hungary's ally Germany declares war on Russia and invades Belgium en route to attacking Russia's ally France.

August 1914

France's ally Britain declares war on Germany and Austria-Hungary.

August 1914

German forces halt Russian advance at the Battle of Tannenburg in East Prussia.

September 1914

British and French troops halt German advance at Battle of the Marne close to Paris.

September 1914

Russian forces driven from Prussia at Battle of the Masurian Lakes.

October 1914

Turkey joins Central Powers against the Allies.

October to November 1914

Stalemate at Battle of Ypres. Entire Western Front settles into lines of opposing trenches.

April 1915

Allied troops, including Australian and New Zealand (ANZAC) forces, attack Turkish forces at Gallipoli. The campaign ends in failure and troops are withdrawn in January 1916.

April 1915

Gas first used by German troops against French at Ypres. Its use by both sides becomes widespread.

April 1915

Italy joins the Allies.

February 1916

The bloodiest battle of the War begins at Verdun. It lasts until December. Neither side gains an advantage.

May 1916

The greatest sea battle of the War, at Jutland, takes place over May 31 - June 1. Ends in stalemate.

June to September 1916

Russia makes substantial gains against Austro-Hungarian forces during the *Brusilov Offensive*.

July 1916

The Battle of the Somme begins, with massive British casualties. It ends in stalemate in November.

February 1917

German submarines begin to attack all ships sailing to Allied ports.

March 1917

Russian Tsar Nicholas II abdicates following riots in St. Petersburg.

April 1917

President Woodrow Wilson brings the USA into the War on the Allied side.

April to June 1917

Following another disastrous and costly offensive at Chemin des Dames, French troops mutiny. The revolt is brought under control by new commander in chief Philippe Pétain.

July to November 1917

Another bloodbath at the 3rd Battle of Ypres, in Belgium, which also ends in stalemate.

October 1917

Bolsheviks declare themselves rulers of Russia, which will remain a communist state until 1991.

November 1917

Allied tanks used with great success at Cambrai.

December 1917

British and Arab forces seize Jerusalem from Ottoman Turks.

March 1918

Bolshevik Russia hands over western territory to Central Powers at Treaty of Brest Litovsk, which formally ends the War in the East.

March to June 1918

German Spring Offensive breaks through Allied lines and almost reaches Paris before it runs out of steam.

July 1918

Murder of Tsar Nicholas II and his family by Bolshevik forces.

August 1918

Allied troops break through German lines at Amiens.

September 1918

American troops break through German lines in the Argonne.

The Hindenburg Line is breached and Allied troops head for German border.

November 1918

German forces continue an orderly retreat, but the Home Front collapses with riots and a navy mutiny. The Kaiser abdicates.

November 1918

German government signs a ceasefire at Compiègne forest. The War ends at 11:00 on November 11.

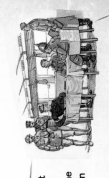

Glossary

This glossary explains some of the words you may come across when reading about the First World War. Words in *italics* have their own separate entries.

airship A large gas-filled aircraft capable of reaching high altitudes.

alliance An agreement between two or more countries to work together.

Allies The nations who fought against the *Central Powers*. The main Allied powers were Britain and its empire, France, Russia and the United States.

anarchist A person who doesn't believe in government of any form.

annex To occupy a country against its will.

ANZACs Soldiers from Australia and New Zealand.

armaments The weapons and *munitions* used by a military force.

armistice An agreement between two or more armies to stop attacking each other.

arms race A race between two or more countries to build more and more powerful weapons.

artillery Large, heavy guns, such as cannons.

auxiliary A person who works to support the armed forces, but isn't directly engaged in combat.

Balkans The countries that lie between Russia, Austria-Hungary and Turkey, such as Serbia.

barbed wire Spiky wire used to defend *trenches*.

barrage A large number of shells fired continuously for a sustained period.

battalion A unit in the armed forces, comprising a large number of soldiers who are organized into several different units.

battleship A large, armed and fortified warship.

biplane A plane with two sets of wings.

bloc A group of countries bound by an alliance.

blockade A military tactic in which an army or navy surrounds a city to stop food and resources from going in or out.

bombardment See *barrage*

cavalry Army units mounted on horseback.

caterpillar tracks A looped track on a tank which helps it to travel over soft or uneven ground.

Central Powers The nations who opposed the Allies. The main Central Powers were Germany, Austria-Hungary and Turkey.

chain reaction A series of events in which each one leads to another.

civil war A war in which armies from the same country fight each other.

civilian Anyone who is not a member of the armed forces.

colony A geographical area under the political control of another country.

Commonwealth The association of countries which were formerly members of the British *empire*.

communism A political system in which the state controls the wealth and industry on behalf of the people. People who follow this system are called communists.

convoy ships Merchant ships that travel in a group, with warships to protect them from attack.

creeping barrage A *barrage* which moves steadily deeper into enemy territory. Footsoldiers advance behind the shelling, which provides cover to protect them from attack.

decipher To decode a message.

depth charge A bomb used to attack *submarines*.

dictator A ruler who imposes his authority by force.

division A large unit in the armed forces made up of a number of *battalions* and brigades.

Eastern Front The boundary between the Russian army and the armies of Germany and Austria-Hungary.

empire A group of countries or territories under the control of another country.

entente A loose agreement between two or more countries that may develop into an *alliance*.

front line The boundary along which opposing armies face each other.

gas attack The release of harmful gas into an enemy position.

garrison A military base or fortification.

genocide A policy of deliberately killing people of a specific nationality or race.

guerilla force A small group of soldiers who use unorthodox tactics, such as ambush.

Hindenburg Line A line of strong German defensive positions along the *Western Front*.

incendiary bullets Bullets that are designed to burst into flames on impact.

jihad A holy war undertaken by Muslims.

Kaiser The emperor of Germany.

League of Nations A diplomatic organization set up after the First World War, for countries to try to settle disputes without resorting to war.

machine gun A gun that can fire bullets very quickly without needing to be reloaded.

mandate Authority given by a peace *treaty* for one nation to take charge of the affairs of another.

memorandum A message or reminder.

military exercises Employing army, navy, or air force personnel in training for military operations.

morale Collective spirit or confidence.

munitions Ammunition, such as bullets, grenades and *shells*.

mutiny A rebellion by soldiers who have lost confidence in their superiors.

Nazi Party The German political party led by Adolf Hitler before and during the Second World War.

No Man's Land The unoccupied area between opposing enemy *trenches*.

occupy To seize and take control of an area.

offensive A major attack.

officer A senior member of the armed forces.

patriotism Loving one's country and being prepared to fight for it.

peninsula A narrow strip of land projecting into a sea or lake.

propaganda Information designed to promote or damage a political cause.

reparations Payments made by Germany to several Allied nations after its defeat in the First World War, justified as being compensation for causing the War.

revolution The overthrow of a leader or government, usually by violent means.

Schlieffen Plan The German plan to attack the Allies through neutral Belgium.

shell A hollow missile containing explosives.

shrapnel Fragments of metal which fly out of a grenade, bomb or shell when it explodes.

sniper A rifleman or woman who takes shots at enemy soldiers from a concealed position.

stalemate A situation where neither side can win, and no further action can be taken.

stormtroopers Highly trained German soldiers who specialized in rapid attacks on particular targets.

straits A narrow channel between two seas.

submarine A ship which can travel underwater for long periods.

suffragettes People who campaigned for women's right to vote.

terrorist A person who commits a violent crime with a political motive.

torpedo A self-propelled, explosive device which travels through water and can be launched from a plane, ship or submarine.

treaty An agreement between countries.

trench A ditch dug as a defensive fortification. Fighting between armies in trenches is known as trench warfare. This applied to most battles in the First World War.

truce A temporary agreement in which two sides agree not to attack each other.

Tsar The emperor of Russia.

U-boat A German *submarine*. From 'Unterseeboot', which means 'undersea boat' in German.

Western Front The boundary between the German army and the armies of France, Belgium, Britain and USA.

zeppelin A large German *airship*.

Index

Acknowledgements

Every effort has been made to trace and acknowledge ownership of copyright. If any rights have been omitted, the publishers offer to rectify this in any future editions following notification. The publishers are grateful to the following individuals and organizations for their permission to reproduce material on the following pages: t=top, m=middle, b=bottom; r=right, l=left

Front and back Cover The Menin Road by Paul Nash, 1919, © IWM ART 2242; **1** © Underwood & Underwood/ Underwood & Underwood/Corbis; **2-3** From a Front Line Trench, from British Artists at the Front, Continuation of The Western Front, 1918 (colour litho), Nevinson, Christopher Richard Wynne (1889-1946)/Private Collection/The Stapleton Collection/The Bridgeman Art Library, © Nevinson/Bridgeman 2013; **4-5** © IWM E(AUS) 1233; **6-7** © Museum of Flight/Corbis; **10-11** © George Eastman House/Archive Photos/Getty Images; **12** © Victoria and Albert Museum, London; **13** © Prisma Bildagentur AG/Alamy; **14-15** © IWM Q 21184; **16 tl** © Bibliothèque Nationale, Paris, France/Giraudon/The Bridgeman Art Library; **16 b** akg-images; **17** © Christel Gerstenberg/Corbis; **18** © Bettmann/Corbis; **19 br** Copyright A J P Taylor, extract from The First World War- An Illustrated History, Penguin, by kind permission; **20-21** © Archives Larousse, Paris, France/Giraudon/The Bridgeman Art Library; **22-23** © IWM Q 53446; **24** The Print Collector/HIP/TopFoto; **25** © Hulton Archive/Getty Images; **26 b** © Mary Evans/Alamy; **27 bl** © The Art Archive/Alamy; **27 br** Library of Congress; **28** © Corbis; **29** Wire, Paul Nash, drawing, 1918, © IWM ART 2705; **30** © IWM Q 70075; **31** © IWM Q 50719; **32-33** © IWM Q 58459; **34** Oppy Wood, 1917. Evening by John Nash, 1918 © IWM ART 2243; **37** AP/Press Association Images; **38-39** Gassed by John Singer Sargent, 1919, © IWM ART 1460; **40-41** © Corbis; **41 br** © IWM PST 12232; **42 l** Mary Evans/The National Archives, London. England.; **42-43 b** © MPI/Archive Photos/Getty Images; **43 tr** © Lordprice Collection/Alamy; **44-45** Roger-Viollet/ Topfoto; **46-47** Mary Evans/SZ Photo/Scherl; **48-49** © Look and Learn/The Bridgeman Art Library; **50** © IWM PST 3283; **51 t** © IWM Q 106249; **51 br** Library of Congress; **52 tl** RIA Novosti; **53 t** © ullsteinbild/TopFoto; **53 br** Library of Congress; **54-55** © Royal Naval Museum, Portsmouth, Hampshire, UK/The Bridgeman Art Library; **56 l** © IWM PST 2734; **56-57 b** © IWM Q1567 & Q1568; **58 t** © 2013. Photo Scala, Florence; **58 bl** © Galerie Bilderwelt/ The Bridgeman Art Library; **59 tr** © IWM ART 2473; **59 b** Library of Congress; **60-61** © IWM E(AUS) 1220; **62** RIA Novosti/The Bridgeman Art Library; **63** © Universal Images Group/Getty Images; **64** © Mondadori/Getty Images; **65 t** © Topical Press Agency/Getty Images; **65 r** Private Collection/The Bridgeman Art Library; **66 bl** Peter Newark Military Pictures/The Bridgeman Art Library; **66 bm** Library of Congress; **66 br** Deutsches Historisches Museum, Berlin, Germany/© DHM/The Bridgeman Art Library; **67 r** Library of Congress; **67 b** © Corbis; **68-69** © IWM Q 9364; **70 t** The Menin Road by Paul Nash, 1919, © IWM ART 2242; **71 b** Canadian Headquarters Staff, 1918 by Sir William Nicholson © Canadian War Museum, Ottawa, Canada/The Bridgeman Art Library; **72-73** © dpa picture alliance/Alamy; **74-75** © IWM Q 55020; **76-77** © Australian War Memorial; **78** © Berliner Verlag/Archiv/dpa/ Corbis; **79** © Popperfoto/Getty Images; **80-81** © Topical Press Agency/Getty Images; **83 tr** Mary Evans Picture Library; **83 b** Signing of the Peace in the Hall of Mirrors, William Orpen, painting, 1919, © IWM ART 2856; **86 tl** Copyright Siegfried Sassoon by kind permission of the Estate of George Sassoon; **86-87 b** © Maurice Crooks/Alamy; **87 t** War Cripples 1920 by Otto Dix, © INTERFOTO/Alamy, © DACS 2013; **88 tr** © Hulton Deutches Collection/ Corbis; **88 l** Roger Viollet/Getty Images; **88 br** © Fine Art Images/Heritage-Images/TopFoto; **89 tl** © Underwood & Underwood/Underwood & Underwood/Corbis; **89 r** © Popperfoto/Getty Images; **89 bl** © Roper/Hulton Archive/ Getty Images. Cover US edition: tl (Sopwith camel plane) © Jim Tannick/Getty Images; tr (Dardenelles map) © Universal Images Group/Getty Images; mr (Poppy) © iStockphoto/Thinkstock; b (German Spring Offensive) © IWM Q 55483

Picture research by Ruth King   Digital manipulation by John Russell

With thanks to Madeleine James, Imperial War Museums